WHOLE
HEARTED

*A Biblical Look at the
Greatest Commandment
and Personal Wealth*

Scott Redd

INSTITUTE FOR
FAITH, WORK
& ECONOMICS

First Edition, 2016

ISBN 978-0-9964257-6-6

Published by the

Institute for Faith, Work & Economics

8400 Westpark Drive

Suite 100

McLean, Virginia 22102

www.tifwe.org

Printed in the United States of America

WHOLE HEARTED

*A Biblical Look at the
Greatest Commandment
and Personal Wealth*

FOREWORD

Dr. Art Lindsley

I have heard that spiritual decline starts in "false-centeredness" – when we put someone or something at the center of our lives that ought not to be there. We can also make some aspect of our faith the center that ought not to be. For instance, we could make eschatology (study of the end times) the center of our preoccupation and even if we were perfectly right in mapping out an end times scenario doctrinally, after a while it would become unhealthy because we would be neglecting the gospel – Jesus Christ crucified and risen. Jesus ought to be at the center of our lives. That is certain.

But does Jesus point us to certain central emphases on which we ought to focus our attention? There are two – the Great Commission (Matt. 28:18-20) and the Great Commandment (Matt. 22:37-40). The first calls us to make disciples of all nations, baptizing them and teaching them to observe all that he commanded them. What is to be central to that teaching? Jesus says that the Great Commandment to love God with all our heart, soul, mind, and strength is the first in priority, and the second is to love our neighbors as ourselves. He says this call to love God is the "great and foremost commandment." This command comes from Deuteronomy 6:4-5 and is sometimes called the "Shema", coming from the first Hebrew word in verse 4, meaning "hear." Israel is called: "Hear, O Israel: The LORD our God, the LORD is one. You shall love the LORD your God with all your heart..."

Dr. Scott Redd, president of Reformed Theological Seminary, Washington, D.C., has written an illuminating study of the Shema that will enlarge your understanding of this central text, and it will impact your life if you let it. Dr. Redd first sets the Shema in its historical and biblical context, then expounds what it means to love God with "heart, self and strength." You will find particularly striking the discussion of the meaning of the word "strength" as the effect a person has on the world around them. Its early interpreters included military might, offspring, farming, wealth and prosperity within the meaning of the word. Thus the Shema moves from the inner person (heart and self) outward to include all of our lives (strength).

This has significant implications on how we steward everything that we have been given, including our wealth. Wealth is both a gift and a challenge – a gift from God (if obtained justly) and a challenge because we can wrongly place it at the center of our lives in various ways. Dr. Redd develops this idea and applies it in a case study of Solomon, who started out with whole-hearted commitment but tragically ended with a divided heart. He allowed the worship of idols, engaged in many marriages to foreign wives, and became consumed with his wealth (contrary to Deuteronomy 7:17). Solomon misused his wealth, his position, his God-given wisdom – all his "strength" for other gods. Solomon's divided heart also led to a divided kingdom.

This study will stretch your understanding and challenge your heart to live a "whole-hearted" life in relationship to God, others, and with all your property and wealth. C.S. Lewis argues that in order to rightly enjoy second things you have to keep first things first. That means having a true centeredness on Jesus and on what he calls us to do. ■

WHOLE HEARTED

A Biblical Look at the Greatest Commandment and Personal Wealth

—■—

Scott Redd

"Hear, O Israel: The LORD is our God, the LORD is one.
You shall love the LORD your God with all your heart
and with all your self and with all your strength."

— Deuteronomy 6:4–5 (author's translation)

When reading this well-known Old Testament creed, traditionally referred to as the "Shema" (shə-MAW) after its first word, the Hebrew imperative verb meaning "hear," there is a temptation to understand these three categories, "heart, self, and strength," as discrete elements of the human nature. For good or for ill this passage is often employed in discussions about the nature of human life and its composite parts, a topic of no small importance and possibly within the purview of the passage at hand, but also probably of secondary concern. This passage says less about the individual, discrete elements of the human being and more about the thorough-going, outwardly directed character of the covenantal love that is required in response to the character of God.

This essay will discuss the biblical emphasis on the commitment of the whole person to the kingdom of God through a process that begins with the inner person and extends outwardly to human effort, relationship, property, and wealth. In the theology of the Shema and the Scriptures as a whole, the use and investment of personal property cannot be divorced from the disposition of the heart. As a result, wealth in itself is never described as morally evil, but rather as a gift of God, which must be managed and disbursed in a way that is commensurate with a faithful heart and mindful of the purposes of the kingdom of God.

This essay will also explore the concept of biblical covenant as it is found in the book of Deuteronomy, show how it finds expression in the Shema, as well as how the rest of the Scriptures, including the teachings of Christ, apply it to the topic of personal wealth.

Deuteronomy as a Covenant Document

It has long been known that Deuteronomy shares features with various covenant documents from the ancient Near East, documents which came to light over the past century. In such documents, vassal kings would swear allegiance to a suzerain in exchange for the benefits of an alliance, including protection and provision.

Two main types of treaties influence the reading of Deuteronomy, those that emerge from the Hittite Empire and those that arise from the Neo-Assyrian Empire, and these two have bearing on the question of dating. If the text can be shown to share elements of Hittite documents, then such a connection would corroborate a dating of the text in the second millennium BC (in the time of Moses). If, however, the text shares features with Neo-Assyrian documents, then this would fit more with seventh century dating. The theory of Neo-Assyrian influence has received the support of scholarly consensus in recent decades, though there have been some efforts to revive the theory of Hittite influence.[1] The discussion is not an insignificant matter. If the Hittite connection can be proved, then the seventh century dating falls, thereby abolishing "an Archimedian point [that critical] scholars use to date other biblical texts."[2] It does not work the other way, however, since any connection between Deuteronomy and the Neo-Assyrian treaty format (especially in Deuteronomy 28) might be construed as an editorial change or update of an older document. In fact, scholars like Levinson and Stackert contend that Deuteronomy may likely contain "multiple treaty influences that themselves differ in significant ways."[3] As a result, the discussion of treaty type will not settle the matter of date for us by itself.

Inner-biblical evidence, such as the testimony in the text of Deuteronomy itself (1:1; 4:44-45; 5:1; 29:1; 31:1; especially 31:9) and the Old and the New Testament attributions of the book to Moses (2 Chron. 35:12; Ezra 3:2; 6:18; and Neh. 8:1; 13:1; Mark 7:10; John 5:46; 7:19; [cf. Luke 24:44]; Rom. 10:5 and 1 Cor. 9:9), assumes a second millennium dating for the addresses found in the book. This dating is corroborated by the emphasis that the book puts on the future life of the nation in the land of Canaan. Extra-biblical evidence also corroborates this early dating due to the unique similarities between the book and second millennium Hittite treaties, including, for instance, the emphasis on the vassal king's (Israel) love in response to the suzerain's (Yahweh) faithfulness and benevolence,[4] as well as the requirement that the vassal and the suzerain both retain copies of the document. Such features are not common to the later neo-Assyrian documents, though the requirement of love toward the sovereign is mentioned in one significant treaty from this time.[5]

Not surprisingly the discovery of ancient Near Eastern treaty documents had profound effects on the study of the structure of Deuteronomy.[6] While the elements differ slightly, the basic format found in extra-biblical covenants sheds light on the outline of Deuteronomy. The outline emerges as follows:

1. Historical Prologue (Deut. 1:1-4:43), in which the past benevolence of the suzerain is rehearsed as the foundation for the covenant relationship.

2. Stipulations (Deut. 4:44-26:19), in which the terms of the covenant arrangement are expressed in full.

3. Provisions for Storage and Periodic Reading (Deut. 31:9-13), in which arrangements are made for the safeguard of the covenant document for future generations.

4. List of Witnesses (no clear parallel in Deuteronomy, though witnesses are mentioned in ceremonial summons [Deut. 30:19-20] and the Song of Moses [Deut. 32:1,43]), in which appropriate witness are identified to testify to the covenant's terms and ratification.

5. Blessings and Curses (Deut. 27-28), in which the consequences of covenant breaking are explained as possible future events.

These elements can be varied in their placement, as can be seen in the similarities identified above. Nevertheless, the outline of the book loosely follows the format of an ancient treaty while maintaining its own unique elements. For instance, the surface arrangement of the book presents the covenant elements in the form of several public addresses given by Moses, the covenant administrator, who leaves his personal and autobiographical marks in the text, referring to himself and giving his own evaluation of the material. McConville is certainly correct in his opinion that the book presents an anthology of "preached law" and that the format of the treaty, as it is currently understood, seems to be employed rather "freely."[7] The covenant law found in Deuteronomy is at once political and pedagogical, legislative and homiletic. While the book has national implications (which are applied in Israelite's history), it also serves the purpose of instructing the individual in the ways of the Lord, how they ought to love him, and what that means for their life in the land.

The Shema

The reader will note that the passage in question, the Shema (Deut. 6:4-9), falls within the beginning of the section dealing with covenant stipulations (4:44-26:19). Kaufman[8] has shown how the order and content of the ten commandments set the structural agenda for this section, and his proposal still stands, though there has been some debate over how the expositions of the commandments are divided in the rest of the book. The outline of the commandments and the corresponding sections of Deuteronomy follow the divisions proposed by Walton with minor modifications.[9]

1. First commandment: Monotheism (Exod. 20:2; Deut. 5:7).
   Exposition: Deuteronomy 6-11.

2. Second commandment: Worship (Exod. 20:4-6; Deut. 5:8-10).
   Exposition: Deuteronomy 12.

3. Third commandment: Honoring the Name (Exod. 20:7; Deut. 5:11).
   Exposition: Deuteronomy 13:1-14:21.

4. Fourth commandment: Sabbath Observance (Exod. 20:8-11; Deut.
   5:12-15). Exposition: Deuteronomy 14:22-16:17.

5. Fifth commandment: Communal Authority (Exod. 20:12; Deut. 5:16).
   Exposition: Deuteronomy 16:18-18:22.

6. Sixth to Eighth commandments: Human Dignity (Exod. 20:13-15;
   Deut. 5:17). Exposition: Deuteronomy 19:1-22:12.

7. Seventh commandment: Sexual Fidelity (Deut. 5:18).
   Exposition: Deuteronomy 22:13-23:18.

8. Eighth commandment: Personal Property (Deut. 5:19).
   Exposition: Deut. 23:19-24:22.

9. Ninth commandment: Truthfulness (Deut. 5:8-10; Deut. 5:20).
   Exposition: Deuteronmy 25:1-19.

10. Tenth commandment: Contentment (Exod. 20:17; Deut. 5:21).
    Exposition: Deut. 26:1-15; Formal conclusion (Deut. 26:16-19).

In this understanding the Shema is located in the section dedicated to the exposition of the first commandment to honor the monotheistic character of the covenant Lord (Deut. 6-11). The section is framed by the repetition of the command to put the words on the heart, bind them to the person, teach them to one's children, and mark them on one's property, given at the outset of the section (Deut. 6:6-9) and at its closure (Deut. 11:18-20).

The logic of the Shema works from the character of God to the proper response of the people who enter into covenant with him. The divine source and the human response are similar in type, reflecting one another so that the response ought to be appropriate in light of the character of God. Regardless of how the propositions of verse 4 are parsed ("The Lord our God, The Lord is one." "The Lord our God is Lord alone." "The Lord Our God is the one

Lord." "The Lord is our God. The Lord is one"), two theological doctrines about the character of God move to the foreground. In the first doctrine, his covenantal relationship to Israel is stated: he is "our God." This means that he is the Lord of their ancestors, Abraham, Isaac, and Jacob, the Lord of their deliverance from national slavery in Egypt, the Lord of their nomadic wandering, and the Lord of their future conquest of the Land. In the second doctrine, his singular character is stated: he is not a regional deity, whose jurisdiction is limited to a geographical location, such as a town or region (for an example of regional deity, see "Baal of Peor" in Num. 25:3-5; Deut. 4:3; Ps. 106:28). The oneness of the Lord contrasts with the plurality of other gods. Israel should not concern itself with a pantheon of deities but with a unified and singular Lord. The exclusivity of the Lord for Israel is not explicitly stated here, but this confession lays the groundwork for other claims of exclusivity found in the Scriptures (Deut. 4:35, 39; also 1 Kings 8:60; 2 Kings 19:15, 19; Isa. 44:5-6; 45:6, 14, 18, 22; 46:9).[10]

These two doctrines of God, his covenantal nature and his unity, lead to the requirement of his people. Because of his covenantal nature, a response is required. Because of his unity, a unified response that includes the whole of the person is required. In a word, that response is "love," a requirement that is evocative of familial language common to ancient Near Eastern covenant documents. Cross has shown how covenants are often described as kinship-making arrangements, expressed both in terms of father-son and husband-wife relations.[11] Such language is not infrequent in describing the relationship between the Lord and his people, both as father-son (Exod. 4:22; Deut 1:31; 8:5; Hosea 11:1) and husband-wife (Hosea; Jer. 2:2; Ezek. 16; Eph. 5). Israel's covenantal-familial love for the Lord should be whole and unified across all aspects of their life, heart, self, and strength.

The spheres of life demarcated by the words, "heart, self, and strength" should be analyzed first individually and then as a whole range. Apart from a few uses of the Hebrew word *lev,* which is translated "heart," in death accounts (1 Sam. 25:37; 2 Kings 9:24), the word does not typically refer to the actual human organ, but rather to the inner space of a place ("heart of the sea" Exod. 15:8; "heart of heaven" Deut. 4:11) or person.[12] When used to describe the inner parts of the human life, "heart" often refers to the general cognitive and volitional capacities of the person (in the Hebrew lexicon there was not a clear distinction between heart and mind in the rationalistic sense). Emotions, desires, and human will emit from the heart of a person. When Hannah's prayer is heard, her heart rejoices (1 Sam. 2:1). When a person fears, his heart "goes out" (Gen. 42:28) or "falls" (1 Sam. 17:32). The heart holds cognitive functions as well, storing up the wisdom that guides the sage (1 Kings 3:12; 2 Chron. 9:23; Prov. 16:23), and is the source of plans and consent, as in "setting one's heart on something" (of the Lord, Deut. 10:15; Job 7:17; 34:14; of humans, 1 Chron. 22:19; 2 Chron. 2:14; 19:3; Ezra 7:10). Finally, the heart provides the moral compass from which a person acts in the world, either for good (Job 11:13) or evil (Jer. 17:9). We ought not look for fine distinction here between emotional and rational faculties since such a distinction would be anachronistic to the conception of the inner person displayed in much of the Old Testament. Such distinctions do occur in the New Testament, however, as might be the case in Jesus' use of the Shema in his own teaching (Mark 12:30; Luke 10:27). In both of these cases, the word "mind" (*dianoia*) is added to the passage, possibly as an exposition of the word "heart" according to Hellenistic norms. Furthermore, the conjoining thoughts and desires in the one category of the heart finds expression in Hebrew 4:12, where the "thoughts/intentions of the heart" are listed as one of three parts of a person, the other two being "soul/spirit," "joints/marrow." The heart is the seat of the inner person, the core of their inner life out of which the rest of their existence springs.

The word *nefesh* (translated "self" above) speaks to the person, the self, perhaps the whole of the living person *as* a person. Like "heart," this term can refer merely to the inner parts of a person, as in the feelings, conscience or appetite, a meaning derived from its basic sense of "throat" or "breath," but it is here disambiguated from the heart, which has led to the use of "soul" that is common in modern English translations of Deuteronomy 6:4-5.[13] The term can be used to refer to the whole of a person, the personality, or the self, and is found in reflexive constructions meaning "to do something to oneself" (Num. 30:5; 1 Sam. 18:3; Isa. 53:10). Thus, the "self" can refer to the whole of the person as they are, including the body. If the heart refers to the inner person, the soul refers to the whole of the person, including the outer body.

The last Hebrew word *meod* (translated often as "strength" or "might") presents a bit of a dilemma, not because it is an uncommon word, but because it is rarely ever used as a noun as it is here.[14] The only other place it is used in this way is 2 Kings 23:25 where the Shema is being quoted to describe Josiah. The word usually occurs as an adverb meaning "very" or "really," but the use here requires some comparison with the ancient translations. The Old Greek translation of this passage uses the word *dunamis,* which means "power" or "strength," while both Mark and Luke (Mark 12:30; Luke 10:27) use *ischus,* which has a similar meaning.[15] Both words have the sense of power in abstraction, though they can also be used to talk about power that has effect in the physical world, as in cases like Exodus 12:41 where "power" (*dunamis*) is used to refer to the divine army, or in Numbers 2:4-28, where the same word is used to refer to the Israelite encampments. Likewise, in the case of Genesis 49:3, "might" (*ischus*) is used to refer to a firstborn child; in Leviticus 26:20, the same is used to refer to efforts to farm the land; and in Deuteronomy 8:17, it refers to one's might in multiplying property. Several Aramaic commentaries, known as targums, translate Deuteronomy 6:5 in a way that corroborates this idea of "strength" referring to the effect of the person in the world around them. The earliest of these, *Targum Onqelos,* renders the strength explicitly as "property,"[16] while *Targum Neofiti* renders it with the known (but not necessarily pejorative!) Aramaic word *mammon* meaning "money." Finally, the Syriac translation reflects similar precision in interpretation with the term *qanin,* meaning "possessions."[17]

Given the wide range of interpretations of the Hebrew word *meod* among its ancient interpreters, including New Testament readers, we must be careful how to proceed. Each of the early interpreters understood "strength" in concrete, physical terms, possibly including military strength, offspring, farming, and explicitly meaning property and wealth. If we take these witnesses as a whole, the strength in view in Deuteronomy 6:5 would refer to what I have called "worldly effect," the consequence of a person's life, one's relational, intellectual, and financial capital as well as influence and impact in the world, or what has been referred to as "estate."

Such an interpretation makes further sense when we see a movement in the teaching from thought to self to activity, from inner person to outer person and finally to effect in the world. This movement is precisely what we find in the following four verses of the Shema (Deut. 6:6-9). The command to love the Lord with the whole of the person ("heart, self, strength") is applied in practical ways to the inner person through memorization ("the words that I command you today shall be on your heart," 6:6), to the self, binding the words to the body (6:8), and to the outward *effect* in the world, including one's children and household (6:7), as well as one's property (6:9) (see Fig. 1).

In other words, the Israelites entering into covenant with the Lord are not meant to dwell on the heart, self, and strength as discrete, independent parts but rather on the whole, the entirety, of human existence. The heart–self– effect/strength dynamic describes concentric spheres emanating out from the inner person to the world around them.

The entirety of the person is to be enamored with the Lord who is one. There is no internal differentiation. There are no free states within the kingdom of the self, but rather they are all devoted to the Lord God. The covenantal love that finds expression must infiltrate and fill the symbolic space of the self, just as the glory cloud filled the tabernacle, chasing out whoever lingered there (Exod 40:34-35).

FIG. 1

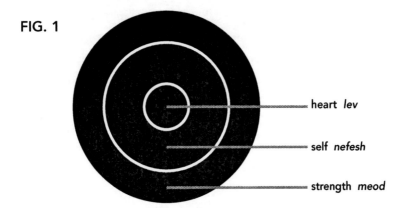

heart *lev*

self *nefesh*

strength *meod*

Wealth as a Divine Blessing and Caution

Understood in light of the covenantal context of the book of Deuteronomy, the Lord's identity as covenant party and unified deity had ramifications for Israel that included every aspect of life, making claims on the collective, as well as the individual. No one was exempt from the covenant arrangement, from the lowest socio-economic class to the king himself, who was to be reminded that his heart should not "be lifted up above his brothers" (Deut. 17:18-20). All were equal before the Lord and all were required to respond with covenantal faithfulness appropriate to their means. This thorough-going covenantal love undergirded all of the covenantal instructions regarding life in the land. Nurture of the heart ought to find expression in the whole of the person and the person's stewardship of the wealth that the Lord has provided.

In particular, the covenant of Deuteronomy gives expression to a notion that love of God ought to extend to the material realm, and as a result the biblical use of wealth should be marked by generosity, stewardship, and investment, all of which glorifies God and honors others who are made in his image. The ramifications of such an arrangement are far-reaching, but we will focus on two primary implications for the Christian life.

Wealth is not morally evil but rather is a blessing from God. Due to common interpretational errors, the perception has arisen that the Scriptures malign the accrual of wealth as merely a sign of unfaithfulness, but the biblical account does nothing of the sort. Wealth is a gift of God from whom all blessings flow. The cultural mandate, found in Genesis 1:28 and reiterated after the Fall in Genesis 9:1, presupposes that humanity is expected to increase in number and dominion over all of creation as image-bearers of the Lord. Such expansion cannot be accomplished without the accrual of property. Abraham is described as a wealthy businessman whose success was not achieved in spite of his relationship with the Lord but as a result of it (Gen. 24:1). In the same way, the prophetic author of Samuel attributes David's success as a warrior and king to the blessing of the Lord (2 Sam. 5:10; 7:13). When Jesus meets the Roman centurion, he says nothing of the man's military authority and success, opting instead to praise him for his faithfulness (Matt. 8:10). Such accounts of wealth and success can be found throughout the Scriptures.

Biblical wisdom literature provides a plethora of teachings regarding even the most minute aspects of wealth production and management. While many wisdom teachings highlight the dangers that accompany the growth of wealth, wealth as a whole is shown to be one legitimate result of the wise life while poverty is often portrayed as a result of folly. In Proverbs 12:27 the lazy person goes hungry, while the diligent person gains wealth. Likewise, in Proverbs 3:9-10, the one who gives the first of his profits to the Lord will find that the Lord blesses him with disproportionately large abundance as a result. The sage of Proverbs 13:22 praises a man as "good" who leaves an inheritance for his children. The beginning of Psalm 112:1-3, which reads like a wisdom teaching, provides an expansive vision of the blessing that awaits those who fear the Lord:

> Praise the Lord!
>
> Blessed is the man who fears the Lord,
> who greatly delights in his commandments!
>
> His offspring will be mighty in the land;
> the generation of the upright will be blessed.
>
> Wealth and riches are in his house,
> and his righteousness endures forever.

We are right to perceive the logic of the Shema in such passages. The inward reverence of the Lord bears fruit in the outward blessings of wealth in the present and for posterity. The simplistic reading that such passages support a "prosperity gospel" interpretation, in which all faithfulness should result in immediate material wealth, does not stand up to the scrutiny of the Scriptures, which are replete with examples of the faithful who live in poverty either by choice or oppression. What these passages do confirm is that the Lord does acknowledge the faithfulness of his people and will certainly bless them with abundance, including material wealth, as he pleases. As the ancient doxology goes, he is the "God from whom all blessings flow," and that includes material success in this life. As a result, all wealth should be received with a spirit of gratitude and heartfelt worship.

How one uses wealth reveals commitments of one's heart. The passages usually cited as proof that the Scriptures oppose the accrual of wealth must be interpreted in light of these clear passages celebrating wealth of all types. When read in context, it becomes apparent that the passages are not undermining wealth *per se* but rather they are addressing either a wrong fixation on wealth or an oppressing use of it.

As we would expect, biblical wisdom has much to say about the foolish man's fixation on wealth. Those who put their hope in material riches suffer from short-sightedness that ultimately leaves them empty-handed in death (Prov. 11:7; 13:11). Because they trust in stored up wealth and ignore the Lord who provides, the gain from their labor does not pass through the veil of death. The wise person, on the other hand, perceives his material gain in the context of his own mortality, recognizing its value and limitations. In another wisdom psalm, the wise man finds himself defrauded, but he does not despair because of his loss, because he knows that his wealthy oppressor cannot save himself from God with his riches.

> Truly no man can ransom another, or give to God the price of his life,
> for the ransom of their life is costly and can never suffice,
> that he should live on forever and never see the pit.

> For he sees that even the wise die;
>> the fool and the stupid alike must perish
>> and leave their wealth to others.

(Ps. 49:7-10)

The wise man knows that his identity and security is ultimately in the covenant Lord and not in the wealth derived from his work. He practices stewardship with what he has been given, but he will not lose the favor of the Lord if he is defrauded of his property. In fact, his security in light of the covenant means that he can receive his wealth joyfully and celebrate his abundance, because his salvation is not tied up in it.

During his preaching ministry, Jesus spoke frequently on the topic of wealth and the proper use of it, and his teaching was deeply informed by the theology of the Mosaic covenant. He taught that the Shema was the "great commandment" of the Mosaic code (Matt. 22:37; Mark 12:30; cf. Luke 10:27), a point that is relevant to our discussion, and that the secondary commandment is "to love your neighbor as yourself" (Lev. 19:18), which will have ramifications for the use of wealth. A prime example of Christ's teaching on wealth can be found in Matthew 6:19-21 and its related passage in Luke 12:22-34, both of which deal with the value of material wealth in relation to the value of eternal reward. In both cases, the contrast is between that which is temporal and that which is eternal, and this contrast gives meaning to the teaching found in both passages. That is to say that wealth is not being rejected out of hand; wealth can and often is a divine blessing bestowed on those who faithfully pursue God's call in their lives as diligent stewards of their gifts and circumstances. The warning here is against a myopic desire for material gain *at the expense* of eternal reward. Read this way, Jesus is developing the themes that were introduced in Old Testament scriptures like Psalm 49:7-13 and Proverbs 11:7 and 13:11.

In Matthew 6:19-21, Jesus encourages his audience to be singular in their service to the Lord and the heavenly treasures that await those who are citizens of his kingdom. At this point in the Sermon on the Mount, he is describing the radical discipleship that marks the lives of his followers. Like the Israelites receiving the terms of the covenant from Moses, Jesus' followers are to be singular in their devotion. If their energies are devoted merely to amassing wealth, then their love of the Lord is called into question. It is hard not to hear echoes of the Shema in the saying, "For where your treasure is, there your heart will be also" (Matt. 6:21). Those who are wholeheartedly committed to Christ's Lordship will not divide their affections between God and money, but even their wealth will be subordinated to his purposes. Jesus sums up his teaching several verses later: "You cannot serve God and money" (Matt. 6:24).

In the Lukan account, the echo of the Shema is also present (Luke 12:34), though in this context Jesus is comforting those who struggle with lives of worry and anxiety. The passage is preceded by a parable about a rich man who relies on his wealth for lasting security, though he suffers an untimely death and loses it all (12:13-21). Jesus then interprets his parable to the audience, reminding them that the Lord knows their needs and provides for them as he pleases. This divine favor and provision ought to comfort them and protect them from the twin temptations of covetousness on the one hand (see the question in 12:15) and anxiety (12:29). Instead of being dissatisfied about the Lord's provision, they ought to find their security in his favor and therefore enjoy the freedom that comes as a result. This freedom allows them to love the Lord in the way that he requires, with all of their heart, self, and worldly effect. Divine Lordship means freedom from the slavery to little things.[18]

The Gift and the Challenge of Wealth

Throughout the Scriptures, men and women of God encounter wealth of different types. Wealth comes in many forms, whether in reputation, authority, intellect, physical attraction, physical strength, military might, or finances. With each comes significant dividends and opportunity to serve the kingdom of God. The covenants of the Scriptures required a love from God's people that makes claims on all aspects of their lives from the most personal to the most public, and that requirement is most clearly articulated in the Shema of

Deuteronomy 6:4-9. Because of the fall of humanity into sin, however, there is also a constant and persistent pull toward fragmentation, toward a rejection of God and his lordship over the human life. As result, the gift of wealth also presents unique temptation to trust in wealth over and against the provision of God.

Moses recognized this human tendency and warned against it ("Beware lest you say in your heart, 'My power and the might of my hand have gotten me this wealth," Deut. 8:17), and Christ acknowledged the same when he famously referenced the "eye of the needle" (Matt. 19:24; Mark 10:25; Luke 18:25), to which the disciples responded, as many of us would have, "Then who can be saved?" Christ's response is telling, "With man this is impossible, but with God all things are possible" (Matt. 10:26). Without the grace of God showered on us as a result of Christ's life, death, and resurrection, by which our sins are forgiven and we are indwelled by the Holy Spirit, a person's wealth provides little more than false reward. For those who are in Christ, however, the gifts we are given provide us with an opportunity to serve the Lord freely and joyfully to the degree that we are gifted, without the crippling force of covetousness or anxiety. They enjoy the abundance that leaves no room in the human heart for greed or despair. As the apostle John reminds us, "for from his fullness we have all received, grace upon grace." (John 1:16).

CASE STUDY:
The Rise and Fall of King Solomon

As we have seen, the Shema calls for a unified view of the faithful human life, one in which the heart, the self, and the worldly effect of a person are wholly directed by the love of the living God. That includes all kinds of what we typically refer to as capital, whether financial, intellectual, relational, political, artistic, and so on. Apart from Jesus Christ, no character in the Scriptures lives out such wholeness with perfect execution, but we do find in the Scriptures many examples of lives directed toward the Lord for a season. Such examples point us toward the ultimate wholeness of Christ, which is made available to us through our union with him.

Such examples also reveal the far-reaching implications of the teaching of the Shema. The relationship that God makes with his people calls them to the sort of love that transforms not merely their hearts, but their entire lives, including every sphere of life in which they operate. One vivid example can be found in the case of the rise and fall of King Solomon found in 1 Kings 1-11. Solomon presents a remarkable case of both a life lived wholly for God and a life tragically fragmented by divided loves. At his best, Solomon shows how every aspect of life and work can be transformed by the love of God; at his worst, he shows how subtle divisions can sneak into the human endeavor and grow into fissures large enough to divide a kingdom.

This case study will focus on the far-reaching implications of the Shema not only in the life of the individual but in the world in which that individual operates. Because Solomon is king of Israel, his worldly effect extends to the events of Israelite history during and after his reign, an effect that is described in remarkable detail. If Solomon had been a private citizen, we would not find eleven chapters dedicated to his rise and fall, comprised of a detailed account of his work in the world. In other words, it is because of Solomon's position as king of God's chosen people that such a deep case study is possible.

This is not to say that Solomon's story only has relevance for those in political or institutional power; rather, the story of the failed son of David shows us the wondrous heights of faithful love as well as the tragic depths of the divided heart. This story is for leaders and followers, businessmen and laborers, pastors and lay people who would expand their moral imagination to gain a deeper understanding of how the love of God can shape their whole life.

Solomon's Story

As the son of David, Solomon begins his reign with a surplus of hopeful expectation. After all, the covenant between God and his royal father David not only established his familial dynasty forever, but it also promised that a son would be born to David who would succeed in building a temple for the Lord and upon whom the covenant love of the Lord would always rest (2 Sam. 7:12-15). The rising tension of the narrative draws its strength from the question of whether Solomon is the great son of David the people were waiting for. Would he establish the country in security? Would he rule with wisdom instead of violence, like his father David? Would he advance the culture of Israel, increasing her fame and the reputation of her God in the surrounding region? The account of 1 Kings 1-11 sets out to answer these questions.

First, this case study of Solomon's rise and fall will consider the breadth of application we see for the theology of Shema, particularly in terms of worldly effect. Solomon is presented as a wholly devoted follower of the Lord (1 Kings 3:3), and that devotion finds expression in a wide array of activities that extend to dynastic affairs, international relations, social justice, and academia.

Second, we will consider the reason for Solomon's ultimate failure as king: the division of his loyalties among foreign dieties. The fragmentation of Solomon's kingdom is not a result of environmental influences, but rather it mirrors the fragmentation in his own heart.

Solomon's Rise: Whole Heart, Unified Kingdom

To understand the story of Solomon's rise and fall, we need to understand its beginnings. Following the short but intense struggle for the throne with his brother Adonijah, Solomon begins the process of securing his royal position (1 Kings 2). David's dying mandate to his son introduces the Deuteronomic tone of Solomon's ascension:

> Be strong, and show yourself a man, and keep the charge of the LORD your God, walking in his ways and keeping his statutes, his commandments, his rules, and his testimonies, as it is written in the Law of Moses, that you may prosper in all that you do and wherever you turn, that the LORD may establish his word that he spoke concerning me, saying, "If your sons pay close attention to their way, to walk before me in faithfulness with all their heart and with all their soul, you shall not lack a man on the throne of Israel." (1 Kings 2:2-4)

The mandate includes clear echoes of the Deuteronomic law, using the common terms "commandments, rules, and stipulations" to encompass the whole of the tradition passed down from Moses.[19] The passage also introduces the theme of the whole heart and whole self as a model for Solomon's reign (2:4), reminding the reader that Solomon's success or failure as a king will spring from the commitments of his heart and his personal disposition toward the Lord his God.

The events of the following section can best be described as a case study of Solomon's wholehearted devotion to the Lord in the exercise of his worldly effect. The picture that is drawn is that of a faithful king effectively enacting his reign through wise dealings in the areas of statecraft including dynastic affairs, international affairs, social justice, and academia. During his rise, Solomon is commended by the Lord for his covenantal commitment in each of these areas, indicating that they should be evaluated by the reader as positive examples of faithful statecraft.

Worldly Effect #1: Internal Affairs (2:13-46). First Solomon must deal with the four-fold problem of his father's personal affairs, including Adonijah, Abiathar, Joab, and Shimei. In each case, the offending party questioned or otherwise acted presumptuously in regards to the authority of David or his choice for an heir, Solomon. Though difficult for the modern mind, the lack of respect communicated by the actions of these individuals is tantamount to treason, a crime against the state, as well as blasphemy, a crime against the God in whose name the king reigns. Solomon's strict execution of judgment must be understood in light of this theological-political arrangement.[20]

This initial account ends with this affirmation of Solomon's activity: "Thus the kingdom was established in the hands of Solomon" (2:46), indicating that the actions were performed effectively and represent judicious rule. Solomon's reign is established through his strong leadership and delegation of duties.[21]

Worldly Effect #2: Diplomatic Relations (3:1-2). Solomon's wise operation of the kingdom extends to diplomatic relations, in this case concerning Solomon's marriage to the daughter of Pharaoh. While this strategic move could be seen as a seed of the discord that will blossom into disobedience later in his reign,[22] its mention here in a positive retelling of Solomon's ascent and the commendation that "Solomon loved the Lord, walking in the statutes of David his father..." (3:3) suggests that it is to be viewed favorably.[23] Once a small local entity, Israel has now risen to a position of international influence under Solomon's leadership.

Worldly Effect #3: Wise Social Justice (3:3-28). In the dream that occurs during Solomon's stay in Gibeon,[24] the Lord solicits a request from Solomon, and the king shows his true, heartfelt devotion to the Lord by asking for a special measure of wisdom, which the Lord grants. Solomon, now endowed with divinely enhanced wisdom, exhibits a conspicuous shift in behavior by returning to Jerusalem to offer sacrifices before the arc of the covenant.

The story of the dispute between the two mothers (3:16-28) provides an extended account of Solomon's stewardship of this gift of wisdom in the area of social justice. This case highlights the need for wisdom in the work of justice. No amount of covenant observance will help the king get to the bottom of the case, which is ultimately a matter of "she said…she said…" testimonies, but his wisdom in matters of human behavior and affections serves the cause of justice and reveals the false testimony for what it is.

As it is the function of the kingly office to administer justice in the land (a practice that continues today, even in certain democratic government structures; see, for instance the U.S. Department of Justice, and the presidential prerogative to nominate and appoint federal justices), Solomon's wisdom in judicial proceedings credential him for the throne. When the citizens of Israel hear report of his decision, they stand "in awe of the king, because they perceived that the wisdom of God was in him to do justice" (1 Kings 3:28). The life devoted to the love of the Lord will pursue divine wisdom and apply it faithfully.

Having secured his reign from internal threats, established diplomatic presence, and procured a system of justice, Solomon goes about the business of appointing his royal cabinet and tribal governors.[25]

Side-Bar: The Fruit of Dynastic Stability, National Security, and Social Justice (4:20-34). The growth of Judah and Israel in population and wealth as well as the increase of Solomon's reputation for wisdom and insight provides a sense of the extent to which Solomon found success in his reign.[26] While military force can affect geopolitical expansion in brute terms, the success of securing the peace determines whether the expansion was worth it. That is why it is important to note that Solomon's expansion is marked by peaceable relations with the countries' neighbors, and much of his wealth seems derived from both taxation as well as foreign tributes (4:21). Furthermore, Solomon's regional diplomacy is expanded to include a treaty with King Hiram of Tyre, a coastal kingdom to the north of Israel.[27] Paired with the marital bond with Egypt, the relationship with Tyre would shore up control of trade in the eastern Mediterranean and the Levant.[28] Such regional command illustrates how much Solomon excelled in the exercise of statecraft in both domestic and international affairs.[29]

Worldly Effect #4: Academia. Solomon's love of the Lord finds expression in the stewardship of his divinely granted wisdom in the area of intellectual pursuits. This passage highlights his command of the realm of ideas (1 Kings 4:29-34). Egypt's reputation as a center of wisdom scholarship was world renowned and the eastern desert communities were likewise considered the home of an impressive wisdom tradition (Job 1:3; Isa. 2:6; cf. Judg. 6:3, 33; 7:12; Isa. 11:14; Jer. 49:28; Matt. 2:1-12). Notably, Solomon's wisdom surpassed them all.[30] Education fell under the responsibility of the king. In Israel and the ancient Near East, sages operated in the court of the king where their training would be utilized for the sake of the realm.[31] It is significant, therefore, that Solomon shows himself to be a wise king whose ability to shape the life of the mind exceeds the best of sages. He boasts a body of work comprised of 3,000 proverbs and 1,005 poems, and his expert knowledge of the flora and fauna is reminiscent of Adam's kingly duty of naming the animals in the Garden of Eden (Gen. 2:20). The work of classification by naming brings the natural world into order, just as the work of classification of ideas and behavior by speaking in proverbs brings the world of ideas into order. Both of these are kingly duties, extending the dominion of humanity over the creation (Gen. 1:28).

The account of Solomon's early kingdom in 1 Kings 1-4 presents a case study in proper execution of God's provision to bring order to the kingdom of Judah and Israel and all of its affairs, and in doing so Solomon fulfills his calling as a faithful and effective king securing the country as a sanctuary of the Lord in his holy temple. Solomon reigns as his father could not, dispatching internal rivals, expanding the borders of the land, succeeding in international relations, enacting social justice, and expertly ruling over the land as well as the realm of wisdom and ideas. In doing so, he ascends to the literal role of faithful son of David and the typological role of second Adam. Things seem to be going very well for God's people on earth.

Solomon's Fall: Divided Heart, Divided Kingdom

The moral of Solomon's ascension is that when the heart of the king is devoted to the Lord (1 Kings 3:1), that devotion affects every aspect of the king's reign, and the Lord blesses his endeavors in remarkable ways that extend to every aspect of his reign. As the narrative of Solomon continues, the opposite dynamic proves to be true as well. As Solomon's heart reveals subtle fragmentation, his true love of the Lord is contrasted with the false loves of his foreign wives and their idolatrous worship. His divided heart has implications for his ability to direct his worldly effect wholly to the Lord.

Solomon's divided heart becomes evident first in his building agenda for the temple of the Lord in which he prioritizes his own palace at the expense of furnishing the temple. His divided heart is fully revealed through his acceptance of the foreign deities of his many wives. The first evidence has to do with mixed priorities in temple-building; the second has to do with mixed loyalties in worship.

Mixed Priorities in Temple-Building. Solomon's marriage to the daughter of Pharaoh would not fall under the restrictions of Deuteronomic law since she is not a Canaanite (Deut 7:3), but even an authorized marriage can become idolatrous if it is prioritized above the love of the Lord. This point is relevant to the account of Solomon's building of the temple to the Lord. While the building project has a promising start, several complications arise that indicate an internal conflict. The king completes the work on the temple structure in seven years (6:38), but the temple is not furnished and therefore suitable for worship until much later (7:51). In the meantime, Solomon completes work on his own palace complex as well as the palace for his Egyptian wife (7:8).

This delay in the construction of the temple would have presented no small dilemma for the people, since it would have meant that they were forced to continue worship in the high places while the temple sat empty in Jerusalem. Furthermore, Solomon dedicated thirteen years to the work of his own house, a considerable length of time that is contrasted with the seven years required for the building of the house of the Lord. The two timetables are placed side by side to highlight the disparity (6:38-7:1).

After this inauspicious building program, Solomon consecrates the temple for worship and receives a vison from the Lord in which the Lord warns him of the dangers of a divided heart. In the vision, the Lord first reaffirms his covenant with David, but then warns,

> But if you turn aside from following me, you or your children, and do not keep my commandments and my statutes that I have set before you, but go and serve other gods and worship them, then I will cut off Israel from the land that I have given them, and the house that I have consecrated for my name I will cast out of my sight, and Israel will become a proverb and a by-word among all peoples. (1 Kings 9:6-7)

The irony of this passage can be found in the play on words in the last clause. While Solomon's *môšēl* "ruling" (4:21 [5:1]) culminated with his speaking *māšāl* "proverbs" (4:32 [5:12]), unfaithfulness would turn Israel into a *māšāl* "proverb" (9:7) of warning to others. This similar sounding of words (a common literary device in ancient and modern Semitic literature) draws attention to the severe devastation that accompanies turning away from the Lord (cf. Deut. 29:24; Job 17:6; Ps. 69:11; Jer. 22:8-9; Joel 2:17). If wholehearted love for the Lord evokes extravagant blessings, a divided heart evokes extravagant curses.

Mixed Loyalties in Worship. The divine warning foreshadows the tragic denouement of the Solomonic reign, as the hints of his infidelity to the Lord seen in the building of the temple blossoms into full idolatry as a result of Solomon's multitudinous marriages to wives who do not share his covenantal commitments before the Lord. Such lack of constraints in marriage rigorously opposes the teaching of Deuteronomy about royal unions ("And he shall not acquire many wives for himself, lest his heart turn away, nor shall he acquire for himself excessive silver and gold." Deut. 17:17), though Solomon's unfaithfulness is possibly worse, since he is drawn away, not by silver and gold, but by false gods. One senses the language of the Shema easily in the narrator's summary of the situation: "For when Solomon was old his wives turned away his heart after other gods, and his heart was not wholly true to the LORD his God, as was the heart of David his father" (1 Kings 11:4). David was credentialed to the throne because of his heartfelt devotion to the Lord (1 Sam. 13:14; 16:7), but Solomon's divided heart means that the kingdom will be divided as well (1 Kings 11:11-12).

Conclusion

In the story of Solomon's rise and fall, we see a vivid case study in the teaching of the Shema. Solomon understands that his love of the Lord must find application in the ways in which he leads his people and secures their prosperity. As a result, his rise to power is vigorous, innovative, and just. As he pursues the Lord in his statecraft, he finds successes without precedent, but as he succumbs to other loyalties, he fundamentally loses the kingdom he worked so hard to attain. His story reminds us of other tragic stories of leaders, pastors, community leaders, politicians, and others whose early success gave way to public failure. As such, his story should provide one part encouragement and one part warning.

Solomon's rise shows us that we err if we think of the biblical faith as merely a personal, internal activity, with little effect on the world around us. Solomon's fall shows us that the divided heart can result in far-reaching failure and instability (James 1:8).

The teaching of the Shema (Deut. 6:4-9) provides a grand biblical metaethic that can be used to explain many such stories and teachings found in the Scriptures. The inner-outer dynamic that begins with heartfelt love that extends to the whole of the self and the whole of a person's effect in the world finds expression throughout the history of Israel, the preaching of the prophets, and ultimately the character and teaching of the Jesus Christ. When Christ calls the Shema the "greatest commandment" (Matt. 22:34-40), he means it. God has laid claim to the whole of human existence and he means to see that claim fulfilled through the work of salvation. Those who believe are united with Christ, and through the power of his spirit, their hearts are directed daily to the sort of love described in the Deut 6:4-9.

In fact, as "new creations" (2 Cor. 5:17), Christians must recognize that every aspect of human experience falls under the influence of saving faith. Never a small thing in Scripture, this expansive vision of biblical faith leaves no stone unturned, but instead appropriates every inclination, thought, gifting, personal relationship, vocational exercise, and property for the glory of the God who desires our whole affections. Any attempts to minimize this expansive vision or to perforate the human life, creating a division of loyalties, ultimately diminish the gospel of Jesus Christ and the teaching of Scripture. When it comes to the claims of divine lordship, we should not shy away from universals.

The Scriptures call us, as followers of Christ, to a significant paradigm shift. Whether we are blessed with abundant wealth or modest means, we ought to recognize the opportunity available to us to show our love for God in the way that we steward our riches. As we seek to praise the God from whom all blessings flow, and give glory to the Lord from whom and through whom are all things (Rom. 11:36), we can celebrate together that this praise and glory is not merely a private, personal endeavor but one that extends to every aspect of our lives. ■

ENDNOTES

1. See J. Berman, "CTH 133 and the Hittite Provenance of Deuteronomy 13," JBL 131 (2011): 25-44; "Histories Twice Told: Deuteronomy and the Hittite Treaty Prologue Tradition," *JBL* 132 (2013): 229-250; A.Taggert-Cohen, "Biblical *Covenant* and Hittite *išḫiul* Reexamined," VT 61 (2011): 461-88. For a discussion with Berman, see B.M. Levinson and J. Stackert, "Between the Covenant Code and Esarhaddon's Succession Treaty: Deuteronomy 13 and the composition of Deuteronomy," *JAJ* 3 (2012): 133-136; J. Berman, "Historicism and Its Limits: A Respond to Bernard M. Levinson and Jeffrey Stackert," *JAJ* 4 (2013): 297-309; B.M. Levinson and J. Stackert, "The Limitations of >>Resonance<<: A Response to Joshua Berman on Historical and Comparative Method," *JAJ* 4 (2013): 310-33.

2. Levinson and Stackert, "Limitations," 310.

3. Levinson and Stackert, "Between the Covenant Code," 136 (emphasis in original).

4. W.L. Moran, "The Ancient Near Eastern Background of the Love of God in Deuteronomy," *Catholic Biblical Quarterly* 25 (1963), 78-79.

5. J. Lundbom, *Deuteronomy: A Commentary* (Grand Rapids, MI: Eerdmans, 2013). 311.

6. See G. E. Mendenhall, *Law and Covenant in Israel and the Ancient Near East*, 1955; M.G. Kline, *The Treaty of the Great King: the Covenant Structure of Deuteronomy: Studies and Commentary* (Grand Rapids, MI: Eerdmans, 1963); *The Structure of Biblical Authority* (Grand Rapids, MI: 1972); D.J. McCarthy, *Treaty and Covenant* (Analecta biblica 21; Rome: Pontifical Biblical Institute, 1963); K. Baltzer, *The Covenant Formulary*, 1971 (trans. David Green from Das Bundesformular, 1964). See also D.J. Wiseman, "The Vassal-Treaties of Esarhaddon," Iraq 20:1-99 + pls [= *The Vassal-Treaties of Esarhaddon*. London: British School of Archaeology in Iraq, 1958].

7. J.G. McConville, *Deuteronomy* (Downers Grove, IL: InterVarsity, 2002), 24.

8. S.A. Kaufman, "The Structure of the Deuteronomic Law." Maarav 1/2 (1978-79): 105-108.

9. J. Walton, "An Exposition of the Spirit of the Law," Grace Theological Journal 8.2 (1987): 213-25; A. Hill and J. Walton, A Survey of the Old Testament (Grand Rapids, MI: Zondervan, 2009) 169; J. Lundbom, Deuteronomy: A Commentary (Grand Rapids, Mich.: Eerdmans, 2013) 77-78; Walton, "The Decalogue Structure of the Deuteronomic Law," Interpreting Deuteronomy: Issues and Approaches (eds. D. G. Firth and P.S. Johnston; Downer's Grove, IL: InterVarsity, 2012), 93-117.

10. Lundbom, *Deuteronomy*, 310.

11. Frank M. Cross, "Kinship and Covenant in Ancient Israel," in *From Epic to Canon: History and Literature in Ancient Israel* (Baltimore, MD: Johns Hopkins University, 1998), 3-21. See also G.E. Wright, "The Terminology of the Old Testament Religion and Its Significance," *JNES* 1 (1942), 404-414; J.W. McKAy, "Man's Love for God in Deuteronomy and the Father/Teacher—Son/Pupil Relationship," *VT* (22 (1972), 426-35.

12. See also L. Koehler and W. Baumgartner, "בל," *The Hebrew and Aramaic Lexicon of the Old Testament* (vol. 1; Leiden: Brill, 2001) 513-515. This basic meaning of "inner part" or "center" is common to other Semitic languages ("libbu," *The Assyrian Dictionary of the Oriental Institute of the University of* Chicago [vol. 9; eds. A.L Oppenheim, E. Reiner, R.D. Biggs; Chicago: The Oriental Institute, 1973], 169-172; J. Hoftijzer and K Jongeling "lbb," *Dictionary of Northwest Semitic Inscriptions* [Part 1; Leiden: Brill, 1995], 563).

13. Koehler, Baumgartner, "שֶׁפֶנ," 711-713; see also "nāpištu," *The Assyrian Dictionary of the Oriental Institute of the University of Chicago* (vol. 11; eds. E. Reiner, R.D. Biggs; Chicago: The Oriental Institute, 1980), 296-304.

14. Koehler, Baumgartner, "דּאמ," 538-39.

15. W. Bauer, W.F.. Arndt, F.W. Gingrich, and F.W. Danker, "δύναμις," *A Greek-English Lexicon of the New Testament and Other Early Christian Literature* (2nd ed.; Chicago: University of Chicago Press, 1979), 262-263; Bauer, Arndt, Gingrich, Danker, "ἰσχύς," 484.

16. M. Sokoloff, "ויסכנ," *A Dictionary of Jewish Palestinian Aramaic* (2nd ed.; Baltimore, MD: Johns Hopkins University, 2002), 351; Sokoloff. "וממ," 311.

17. L. Costaz, "anynq," *Dictionnaire Syriaque-Francais* (3rd ed.; Beirut: Dar El-Machreq, 2002), 322.

18. The story of the rich ruler (Mark 10:17-31; Luke 18:18-30) addresses the same problem. The rich man valued his wealth more than eternal life, and as a result he gave up the greater treasure for the lesser.

19. For other examples of language of Deuteronomy echoed here, see Deuteronomy 4:29; 6:2; 8:6; 9:5; 11:1; 29:9. For the conditions placed on David and Solomon and their successors, see Ian W. Provan, *1 and 2 Kings* (Peabody, MA: Hendrickson, 1995), 31–32.

20. Given the strict measures of Solomon's rise, McConville perceives a negative nuance in this account, one that subtly mocks the activity of the Solomonic administration. Most of the negative elements McConville highlights, however, can either be explained as common royal practice in the ancient Near Eastern and elsewhere, e.g., executing pretenders to the throne and settling dynastic scores, or as ambiguous activity that is positively glossed in order to present an idealized early reign, e.g., participating in cultic worship in the high places. This is not to say that Solomon's rise does not raise questions, but the early events of his reign found in chs. 1–4 are presented as instances of his superlative achievements. J.G. McConville, *God and Earthly Power: An Old Testament Political Theology.* (London: T&T Clark, 2006), 153.

21. Leithart evokes the idea of Solomon as a type of Adam (for more on this typology, see below) to explain the need for these executions: "David knows that as Solomon takes the throne, the garden house of Israel is threatened by "satans" from the previous generation. First among these is Adonijah, who, satanically enough, attempts to seize the king's bride (2:13–18)." Peter J. Leithart, *1/2 Kings* (Grand Rapids, MI: Brazos, 2006), 37–38.

22. See A. Malamat, "The Kingdom of David and Solomon in Its Contact with Egypt and Aram Naharaim," BA 21 (1958) 96–102; "The First Peace Treaty between Israel and Egypt," *BAR* (1979) 58–61.

23. Deuteronomic law does not forbid exogamous marriage with a non-Canaanite (Deut. 7:3).

24. Because the temple has not yet been built in the city of Jerusalem, Solomon travels to Gibeon to offer sacrifices. The account in 1 Kings does not explain why Gibeon is being used as a cultic site, but a parallel text points out that the tabernacle was set up there even though the arc of the covenant had already been brought to Jerusalem (1 Chron. 1:3–6). The narrator of Kings does not excuse or condemn Solomon for the act of using a cultic center outside Jerusalem, though such a practice will later become a serious offense once the temple is built in Jerusalem.

25. McConville helpfully points out that the lack of mention of a governor in Judah indicates a distinction between Israel and the royal tribe of Judah, though he does acknowledge that the unnamed governor mentioned in 1 Kings 4:19 might possibly a Judahite overseer. McConville, *God and Earthly Power,* 152.

26. The section begins with an assessment of the state of the union, which is remarkably good. The inhabitants of country are numerous, festive, and happy (4:20). The description that Judah and Israel were as populous as the "sand on the seashore" recalls the covenantal promise made to Abraham (Gen. 22:17; cf. Josh. 11:4; Judg. 7:12; 1 Sam. 13:5; 2 Sam. 17:11; Isa. 10:22; Jer. 33:22; Hosea 2:1), while the Chronicler connects the large population to the Davidic covenant (2 Chron. 1:9). Likewise, the borders of the land promised to Abraham are finally achieved during the Solomonic expansion (4:21; cf. Gen. 15:18), signifying the end of the conquest of the Land and ushering in what is perhaps the only true "golden age" of the united kingdoms of Judah and Israel.

27. On the quality of the covenant with Tyre, see F.C. Fensham, "The Treaty between the Israelites and the Tyrians," VTSup 17 (1969): 71–87; H. Donner, "Israel and Tyrus im Zeitalter Davids und Salomos. Zur Gegenseitigen Abhängigkeit von Innen- und Aussenpolitik," *JNSL* 10 (1982):43–52.

28. Sweeney, *I & II Kings,* 102.

29. The matter of the horses (1 Kings 4:26) raises a question since Deuteronomy 17:16 warns against this exact thing. In Deuteronomy the concern is that the redeemed people of God might rely on their Egyptian neighbor, the regional source of horses and the home of their historical slavery, for national security when they should rely on the Lord. Notably, the accrual of horses is not condemned by the narrator here, but rather is listed alongside other expressions of Solomon's success. The danger that such behavior implies is not in view here, but rather will become relevant as the narrative of Solomon's reign continues and his loyalty to the Lord becomes divided.

30. Like the activities described in the previous chapters, wisdom falls solidly in the domain of the royal office. The wordplay between *môšēl* "ruled" (1 Kings 4:21 [5:1]) and *māšāl* "proverb" (1 Kings 4:32 [5:12]) draws the connection between kingly reign and the product of wisdom.

31. R. N. Whybray, "Wisdom Literature in the Reigns of David and Solomon," in *Studies in the Period of David and Solomon and Other Essays,* ed. T. Ishida (Winona Lake, IN: 1982), 13–26; "Sage in the Israelite Royal Court," in *the Sage in Israel and the ancient Near East,* ed. J. G. Gammie, and L. G Perdue (Winona Lake, IN: Eisenbrauns, 1990), 133–39; Ronald J. Williams, "The Sage in Egyptian Literature," ," in *the Sage in Israel and the ancient Near East,* ed. J. G. Gammie, and L. G Perdue (Winona Lake, IN: Eisenbrauns, 1990), 19–30.

ABOUT THE AUTHOR

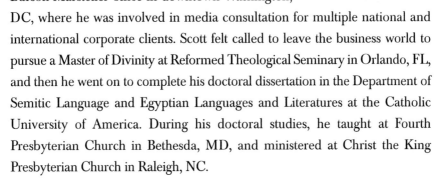

Scott Redd is the president and associate professor of Old Testament at Reformed Theological Seminary in Washington, DC. He began his career at the Burson-Marsteller office in downtown Washington, DC, where he was involved in media consultation for multiple national and international corporate clients. Scott felt called to leave the business world to pursue a Master of Divinity at Reformed Theological Seminary in Orlando, FL, and then he went on to complete his doctoral dissertation in the Department of Semitic Language and Egyptian Languages and Literatures at the Catholic University of America. During his doctoral studies, he taught at Fourth Presbyterian Church in Bethesda, MD, and ministered at Christ the King Presbyterian Church in Raleigh, NC.

In 2009, Scott came back to his alma mater to join the faculty of RTS Orlando, where he also served as dean of students, before moving to Washington, DC, in 2012. Scott has also taught at Catholic University of America, the Augustine Theological Institute in Malta, the International Training Institute, and for Third Millennium Ministries. Scott currently sits on the board of the Washington Theological Consortium, an organization dedicated to ecumenism in the Washington area.

Scott's interests include literary approaches to the Bible, linguistics and the biblical languages, ancient Near Eastern backgrounds to Scripture, and Old Testament theology. He cares deeply about the teaching of Scripture and its application to all situations in life, particularly in the context of a learning and worshiping community. Due to this interest, he continually finds himself drawn to the learning community of the seminary as well as that of the church. Scott lives in Northern Virginia with his wife and five daughters. ∎

ABOUT THE INSTITUTE
FOR FAITH, WORK & ECONOMICS

The Institute for Faith, Work & Economics™ (IFWE) is a non-profit, 501(c)(3) Christian research organization committed to promoting biblical and economic principles that help individuals find fulfillment in their work and contribute to a free and flourishing society.

IFWE's research starts with the belief that the Bible, as the inerrant Word of God, provides the authoritative and intellectual foundation for a proper understanding of work and economic truths that, when properly followed, can help individuals, companies, communities, and nations flourish.

IFWE's research is based on three core principles:
- Each person is created in God's image and, like him, has a desire to be creative and to find **fulfillment** using their God-given talents through work.
- All work, whether paid or volunteer, matters to God, and we as Christians are called to pursue excellence throughout the week – not just on Sundays – stewarding all that we've been given for God's glory and for the **flourishing** of society.
- Therefore, we as citizens must promote an economic environment that not only provides us the **freedom** to pursue our callings and flourish in our work but also reflects the inherent dignity of every human being.

Our desire is to help Christians view their work within the bigger picture of what God is doing in the world. Not only do we help Christians find personal fulfillment, but we also help them understand how to better alleviate poverty, address greed, and view possessions properly. With a biblical view of work and economics, we can partner together to be meaningful participants in God's plan to restore the world the way he intended it to be.

Want to keep reading?

LEARN MORE

If you enjoyed *Wholehearted: A Biblical Look at the Greatest Commandment and Personal Wealth*, you might also enjoy these articles available for free at tifwe.org/research.

"Sell Your Possessions And Give To The Poor":
A Theological Reflection On Jesus' Teaching Regarding Personal Wealth And Charity
by Dr. Jonathan Pennington

Jesus' teachings on wealth and charity draw strong reactions from readers today. Some feel guilty, others get defensive, and a few sell everything. These reactions are all understandable in some ways. Dr. Pennington addresses Jesus' teachings in their historical and modern-day context, reflecting on practical ways to pursue faithfulness in the West today.

— ∎ —

Whole Life Stewardship:
The Call to Greatness
by Dr. Anne Bradley

Most Christians understand a narrow definition of stewardship that only applies to wealth. Biblical stewardship is much more than tithing; it encompasses every single decision we make. Dr. Bradley explores the biblical call to whole-life stewardship.

STORE.TIFWE.ORG

START HERE

The Institute for Faith, Work & Economics provides many resources to help you live a life of freedom, fulfillment, and flourishing. These tools are designed to fit into your life and provide biblical encouragement and guidance to your walk with God.

BLOG
Get our daily or weekly blog updates in your inbox.
BLOG.TIFWE.ORG

RESEARCH
Download free in-depth studies to further your understanding of faith, work, and economics.
RESEARCH.TIFWE.ORG

SOCIALIZE
Connect with IFWE on social media and join the conversation.
FACEBOOK.COM / FAITHWORKECON
TWITTER.COM / FAITHWORKECON

BOOK STORE

Get our latest releases and educational products.

STORE.TIFWE.ORG

DONATE

Become a partner in bringing about flourishing.

DONATE.TIFWE.ORG

PARTICIPATE

Find information about student groups, upcoming events, and other opportunities to get involved.

CONNECT.TIFWE.ORG

INSTITUTE FOR
FAITH, WORK
& ECONOMICS

INSTITUTE FOR
FAITH, WORK
& ECONOMICS